Liner Notes

by

Gary Rainford

Copyright © 2017 by Gary Rainford

All rights reserved. No part of this book may be reproduced or transmitted in any form or by any means without written permission of the author.

ISBN 978-1-943424-21-4

Library of Congress Control Number: 2017941635

North Country Press
Unity, Maine

for Mimi, one ukulele, one trumpet

Thanks to the editors at *The Round Up Writers Zine*, *Ibbetson Street Press*, *The Somerville Times*, and *The Island Reader* where poems in this collection, or earlier versions, originally appeared.

Table of Contents

Abracadabra / 4
Human Behaviour / 5
Blue Skies / 6
12 Stars / 7
Shining Light / 8
My Aim is True / 9
Songbird / 10
Tiger Lily / 11
Weather Systems / 12
Winning Hearts / 13
No Me Quitte Pas / 14
It's Easy / 15
This Voice / 16
Wildwood Flower / 17
American Recordings / 18
Heal the Pain / 19
Sunday Girl / 20
Pure Imagination / 21
Heartbreak Hotel / 22
Higher Ground / 23
Don't Give Up / 24
Saloon Singer / 25
Radio Song / 27
Sacred Heart / 29
Pure Love / 30
Heartbreaker / 33
Ask the Angels / 34
It's Not Unusual / 36
Supernatural / 37
High Flying Bird / 38
Let it Go / 40
Fox Hunting / 41

Water's Edge / 43
Telling Stories / 45
Keep it Open / 47
Through the Years / 48
Single Women / 50
Almost Real / 51
Silver Machine / 52
A No and a Yes / 53
Pale Blue Eyes / 54
My Lady Story / 55
Soul Comes Home / 56
Bad Reputation / 57
Cherish the Day / 58
Slow River / 59
Let Me Fall in Love / 60
Only Love / 61
God / 63
Don't Explain / 65
Last Goodbye / 67
Urge for Going / 68
Sh-Boogie Bop / 69
Blood / 70
Closing Time / 71
32 Flavors / 72
Talking with the Wolves / 74
No Guru, No Method, No Teacher / 75
Sentimental Hygiene / 76
Hero in Me / 78
Beeswing / 79
Psycho Killer / 80
Metamorphosis / 82

CODA:

The Music Never Ends / 84

PRELUDE

Nineteen seventy-six. I am seven years old, the lead singer for the Bay City Rollers. I am standing at the radiator in my bedroom, performing "Saturday Night," our chart busting, pop-rock hit, on the *Tonight Show*.

After keying the last notes on the cold steel radiator pipes, which in my world of make-believe is a Roland SH-5 synthesizer, Johnny Carson invites me to his desk for a short interview. We shake hands. Ed McMahon compliments my plaid leisure suit and spiffy brown leather shoes.

"When did you start writing songs for the Rollers?" Johnny taps a pencil in the air as if he were still singing along.

"Me mum's big joke is at the pubs that I've been composin' since me first coo coo kachoos," I reply, my Scottish accent garbled and more like a New Yorker from Long Island than the tartan teen sensation from Edinburgh.

The live studio audience rock 'n' rolls with laughter.

Johnny and Ed rock 'n' roll too.

Liner Notes, 64 ekphrastic poems, reaches back to this time in my bedroom when music first pierced my skin, the lyrics, "Dancin' to the rhythm in our / Heart and soul / On Saturday night, Saturday night," still playing in my head, fingers still writing and performing songs on that radiator.

Ekphrasis is an ancient practice of using words to describe works of art. The oldest example is *Eikones*, by Philostratus of Lemnos, who lived from 190 – 230 AD. *Eikones,* or

Images, described 64 pictures from a gallery in Naples, Italy.

Ekphrasis is a bit like the art of sampling.

For decades, experimental musicians have created new hit songs by repurposing lyrics or melodies from previous hits. In 1969, "Come Together," by The Beatles sampled, "You Can't Catch Me," by Chuck Berry. In 1989, "Fight the Power," by Public Enemy sampled, "Funky Drummer," by James Brown. "Iron Man," by Black Sabbath was sampled in "Hell of a Life," by Kanye West in 2010. Lady Gaga sampled Queen. Led Zeppelin sampled Muddy Waters. And Pink Floyd sampled Tchaikovsky.

Artists inspire artists, and *Liner Notes*—64 ekphrastic poems describing 64 musicians as artists making music—exemplifies this rich, evocative tradition.

    —Gary Rainford, Swan's Island, Maine, 2016

"Music gives a soul to the universe,
wings to the mind,
flight to the imagination, and life to everything."

–Plato

Abracadabra

Orange and red
hues paint the still sky
like promises.

For only a waking
instant, the moment the
upper limb appears,

"the sun comes
up / And it shines all around
you / You're lost

in space / And the
earth is your own," Steve
Miller glorifies

the U.S. Cellular
Pavilion, Gilford, New
Hampshire,

marquise cut diamond
afterglow in his eyeglasses,
serenity as morning,

and the optical illusion
of Les Paul jazz, electric
guitar virtuosity.

Human Behaviour

Twenty-two hours of day
light in the summer and tireless night
of winter Bjork erupts,

a vivid quirky soprano,
"On the surface simplicity / But the darkest
pit in me / It's pagan

poetry," the blizzards, the icebergs
of blue, ocean, and tree-bare Reykjavik,
where Mother is an island.

Blue Skies

"Summertime," Ella Fitzgerald—
eyes closed and sweat running down
her cheeks—jazzes

every syllable into a thin line
of horn-like phrasing which conveys
a lifetime: her mother's fatal

car accident, her stepfather's
lewd, felonious hands, the Colored
Orphan Asylum in Riverdale,

New York, winning amateur
night at the Apollo Theater, the Decca
years with Dizzy Gillespie

and Louis Armstrong, be-bop,
a Grammy-winning "Mack the Knife"
performance, congestive heart

failure, both legs amputated,
diabetes, her final days wheelchaired
in the backyard of her Beverly Hills

mansion, and her granddaughter.
"I just want to smell the air, listen to the
birds and hear Alice laugh,"

she tells her son, a soft smile on
her face, fish jumpin', the cotton high,
and where the livin' is easy.

12 Stars

Radio City
Music Hall is
on its feet.

White molies
fall from the sky,
center stage.

AGT judges
can't believe
the miracle.

"I don't know
my name," witty
ukulele chords

and the brio
of a 12-year-old
girl, yellow

capris, cute
Taylor Swift bangs
stop the show.

"I don't play
by the rules of
the game,"

Grace blues
the sky, sings her
way found.

Shining Light

Savage as Screamin' Jay
Hawkins, Annie Lennox tears
up the stage. "I put a spell

on you," she swaggers
to the microphone, soulfully
voiced, platinum blond

pixie cut, and a sedge of
flutes fly across the sky, long
legged herons wading

in the bright of Daniel, who
dead at birth sips from another
wellspring where his

mother is a potter shaping
pain into clay into song on *The
Ellen DeGeneres Show.*

My Aim is True

Arrested for busking
outside a London convention
of record executive

muckety-mucks who
wouldn't release his music
for the United States

Elvis Costello alerts
voices in your head, riptides
edgy as protest, decades

later, Orono, ME. "Oh
my baby, baby, I love you more
than I can tell / I don't

think I can live without
you," he rails about romance,
afflictions of infidelity,

Stetson hat, Buddy Holly
glasses, blurred Polaroid man
of singularity.

Songbird

Soft jazzy light
Eva Cassidy shines
on the Blues

Alley supper club,
guitars like church bells,
drums and cymbals

like psalms. "People
get ready / There's a train
a-coming,"

Eva sings her last
set. "You don't need no
baggage / You just

get on board," so
every possible night
she gets on board

once the aching
in her hips is diagnosed
as melanoma that

spreads to her bones.
"All you need is faith / to
hear diesels

humming / You don't
need no ticket / You just
thank the Lord."

Tiger Lily

Metallic gypsy dress,
puffed sleeve blouse, low
neckline, Natalie

Merchant quivers
and quakes, then pleads, "Go
west / Paradise is there

You'll have all
that you can eat / Of milk
and honey over there."

Over 800 fractured miles
in the earth's crust extend along
California's coastline,

a tectonic boundary
between Pacific and North
American plates.

"San Andreas Fault
moved its fingers / Through
the ground / Earth

divided / Plates collided
such an awful sound," Natalie
pours molten rock

into the microphone,
fierce barefoot tremors, land
of delicate dreams.

Weather Systems

Melody desperately searching
for sound, the door slamming one
last time, one last Saturday

night argument too much that
you make sail for good, the swelling
violin the easiest way to express

your frustrations, the dissonance
between your heart and head, Lester
Young to Bartok to Ravel

at your fingers chipping off pieces
of Beethoven to Ramones, pizzicato
skittering, legato textures of

ethnic Romani migration, "And when
you wake up, another sunrise / Another
break up, this ship is capsized,"

oars and plans washed away in
the tradition of no distant homeland
to run to for safety.

Winning Hearts

"I can feel it,"
Neil Diamond, garbed
in rhinestones,

hones the chorus
into sea-glass, and the
crowd adores him;

born in Brooklyn,
1941, Diamond wrote
sweetheart poems

in high-school for
pretty girls he wanted
to impress—song

writing, he says, was
pure passion, his first real
interest, inspired by

Pete Seeger, seeing
him perform at a camp
for Jewish kids,

upstate, New York,
"Makin' time to the beat
of delirious love."

No Me Quitte Pas

"Love me, love me, love me,
say you do," Nina Simone pianos
the keys, trembling; her voice,

between the F below middle C,
is bipolar, pleading with Andrew,
her husband, who protects her

from everybody, but himself;
Lisa, their daughter, recalls blood-
baths, the whiplash-backhands,

the sticks of dynamite and honey
that fueled her mother's love affair
with fire. "Inside I'm screaming,"

diary entries reveal Nina's ruckus
despair, desperate as sleeping pills,
raw as talent, begging for relief.

It's Easy

Fog lifts from
Blue Mountain Peak;
you see Jah

in the sky, feel
Jamaican rhythms
in the trumpet

player's steel-
drum solo. "Words
are few / I have

not spoken / I
could waste a thousand
years," Boy

George sings
a slow, bluesy Black
River flowing

into Lacovia,
barefooted, Rastafari
children dancing.

This Voice

"Words," Ane's lilting, dusky voice
is Maritime, salted melodious mist. "Words, take her
with you / Let her rest in your rhyme."

In 1998 Ane was diagnosed with lupus,
an incurable autoimmune disease, acoustic guitar
foehn wind yoked by rain-shadows of

chords, fingerpicking, and North
Atlantic Drift. Ane describes writing as religious,
an almost religious feeling of disappearing

into creation, awareness greater than suffering.
"Words," a piano rings like the bells at Molde Cathedral
where Ane was born. "Words, ease her

breathing / Lay her softly on the floor,"
and a cello's fretless bass rises from the wood
clad hills. Molde is Old Norse for

fertile soil, rich timpani mallets gathering
the snare drum and cymbals, "Words, help her change
the world / In only one verse."

Wildwood Flower

June Carter Cash plucks
a Grand Ole Opry of heartbreak
on the autoharp.

"There is no way to
be in that kind of hell, no way
to extinguish a flame

that burns, burns, burns,"
June wrote after reading, "Love
is like a burning ring

of desire," underlined
in her uncle's Elizabethan book
of poetry.

American Recordings

Mexican, mariachi-style horns
brass the Grand Ole Opry. "Love
is a burnin' thing," Johnny Cash

confesses wholeheartedly,
a bass-baritone who carries his guitar
as if it were a Tommy Gun

spitting bullets. Johnny's first
wife claims he wrote "Ring of Fire"
drunk and pilled-up, that it's

about betrayal, "Bound by
wild desire," another woman's thighs,
the ride of her breasts,

but their daughter Rosanne, caught
in the barrage, says the song is about
change, the power of love.

Heal the Pain

Cathedral of soul,
post disco dance pop,
and Chopin magic,

George Michael's
voice climbs into the
clouds over Rio,

bursts into rain,
then thunders, "Gone
from painful

cries / Away from
saddened eyes / Along
with them I'll bide,"

but when his lover,
Anselmo, is diagnosed
with HIV, Michael

is afraid for his own
life too, the cold seizures,
the blackouts of blunt

axes, and the shame,
not telling his mother,
who had to believe

her MTV son would
find a worthy woman,
get married.

Sunday Girl

Secretary at BBC Radio,
waitress at Max's, go-go dancer,
Playboy bunny, hyena

Debbie Harry snarls,
tantalizes the live studio dance
audience, "One way

or another I'm gonna
find ya / I'm gonna getcha, getcha,
getcha, getcha . . ."

Inspired by a boyfriend
who stalked her after a breakup
Debbie is not your typical

call 911 victim; she is plastic
thigh-hugging-black-stiletto boots,
she is tight-sassy dress,

midriff missing, she is total
skin power, total crazy-blue eyeliner
as she claws at the TV

camera, Burt Sugarman's
late-night music variety series,
The Midnight Special,

biting, strutting across the
stage, sweet-talking erotomaniacs
with rat food and consent.

Pure Imagination

Hovering mid-air, beating
wings flapping at high frequencies,
ultrasonic-song shakes the

microphone: violin, cello, choir
bell, bassoon, flute, oboe, marimba,
electric guitar, timpani.

Seeking nectar Fiona Apple—
slim shoulders, hollow bones, ruby
throated—feeds at a flower.

Fallen Aztec warriors and
raped 12-year old girls return to earth
as hummingbirds, and sing,

"Be kind to me, or treat me
mean / I'll make the most of it, I'm
an extraordinary machine."

Heartbreak Hotel

"This is a song I
just recorded," Elvis slurs into
the microphone.

Dark-blue eyes separate
from his face, like somebody
heavily drugged.

It's 1977, Rapid City,
South Dakota, six weeks before
he is found dead.

"Is the record out yet?"
Elvis trips over a heap of syllables,
sweating sequins,

but when his fingers chord
the piano and the audience cheers,
a husky voice, smooth as

Kerouac, cancels drug
abuse, and, "Oh, my love, my
darling / I've hungered

for your touch, a long lonely
time / And time goes by, so slowly
and time can do so much."

Higher Ground

One mandolin, two guitars, one cello, one
fiddle, one Arkansas piano accordion, and "Sweet is
the melody, so hard to come by. / It's so hard

to make every note bend just right," admits Iris
Dement, the youngest of thirteen siblings whose mother
postponed Nashville singing aspirations

to raise a Pentecostal family with countrified,
gospel music values. "You lay down the hours and leave
not one trace / But a tune for the dancing is there

in its place," Iris Grand Ole Opries a house
concert, red living room walls, white crown molding,
and her voice is an angel's, twitchy-twangy.

Don't Give Up

Living in the copper timpani
drum's mallet is attack is the story
of coma, police brutality,

protest, twenty-two hours
of deadly interrogation, manacles,
a Land Rover, Stephen Biko,

and 1100 hemorrhaging
kilometers to a prison with hospital
facilities in Pretoria, South

Africa, "September '77 / Port
Elizabeth weather fine / It was business
as usual / In police room 619,"

Peter Gabriel, New Blood
Orchestra, and two backing vocalists
gooseflesh the Live

on David Letterman studio
audience, standing in place, singing
in solidarity, cellphones

flashing pictures and videos,
fists like mallets pumping in 4/4 time,
blindfold, a balance, and sword.

Saloon Singer

Pinkie-ringed and mic'd
after a few too many years
in retirement Sinatra is

black-tuxedo-casual,
The Main Event, a televised
concert, Madison Square

Garden, 1974; the stage
is a boxing ring, a salute to
his father, an illiterate

bantamweight boxer who
fought under the name Marty
O'Brien. "My poor old

heart, it ain't gaining too
much ground," Ol' Blue Eyes
serenades, lights a cigarette,

cups the brief smoke in
his hands; Sinatra's mother
Dolly owned a tavern in

Hoboken, where he sang
songs over the player piano
as a boy for spare change.

"Drink up all of you
people / Order anything you
see / And have fun, lotsa

fun, you lucky people / The
drinks, and the laughs, on me,"
Sinatra's musky voice fades

into the ensemble jazz of
the Young Thundering Herd,
Woody Herman conducting.

Radio Song

Full ascetic beard
Michael Stipe sings David
Bowie, "We met upon

the stair, we spoke of
was and when / Although
I was not there,

he said I was a friend,"
and the pianist ascends the
ice capped Himalayas,

spirit border between
India and Tibet, where sadhus
rises, warm sacred

adagio, and the red
stage lights burn: "I laughed
and shook

his hand / And made my
way back home," Stipe sings
the goddess Sarasvati,

bull-nose ring metal
glinting. *When you know
there is a piece*

*of yourself you haven't put
together yet*, explained Bowie
before he died

during an interview,
you have this great searching,
this great need to find out

who you really are; and
then, Stipe chants into the mic,
sandwind, prayer, and

the grueling grammar of
bliss, those wide-open spaces
between words.

Sacred Heart

Dragons of firelight, black leather
and drama, drums, electric guitars, big 1980s
hair, and the arena is loud,

geological, *furor poeticus*—divine
insanity. "We're the ship without a storm
The cold without the warm / Light

inside the darkness / That it needs,"
Ronnie ballads the stage, sparks flying, classic
Greek theater, live at the Spectrum.

Influenced by American 1950s opera
tenor Mario Lanza, Ronnie popularized throwing
metal horns, a hand gesture

used by artists and fans of heavy metal
music. "We're a laugh without a tear / The hope
without the fear / We are coming, home,"

brute vocals tip centers of gravity, jolts
of iron and steel and brass, electroconvulsive
euphoria.

Ronnie's grandmother dubbed him
Dio, Italian for God, because thunder is sacred,
a gift from God.

Pure Love

"My my my,
it's a beautiful
world / I like

swimming
in the sea," sings
Aaron, grate-

ful, delighted,
floating on his back
out beyond

the white
Hawaiian breakers,
loving the

sapphire blue
moments, the hot
holiday sun

when a shark
bites his baited leg
at the ankle.

Swimming
for the beach,
sunbathers

look on in
terror as the shark
trails him.

"My my my,
it's a beautiful
world,"

he continues
singing, because
he doesn't

know what
else to do except
sing and

swim or freak
out, and Colin Hay,
tuning his guitar,

zesting chords,
improvising, can't
sing this song

without telling
Aaron's story first,
or about being

an alcoholic
expatriate, ex-
Men at Work

lead singer,
how he loves
drinking

but can't
drink or the drink
will kill him.

"My my my,
it's a beautiful
world,"

Colin Hay sings,
and a scruffy smile
that lights

up the stage
finds his magic,
lazy eye.

Heartbreaker

Chunky earphones, tight lattice print
pants sitting cross-legged on a barstool, suede boots,
sprawling black frock, and Juilliard School

aspirations: Pat Benatar trained as coloratura,
a lyric soprano who specializes in florid
vocalization—runs, staccati, wide leaps, and trills,

like Rossini operas. "We belong to the light,
we belong to the thunder," she performs La Cenerentola,
a Cinderella story, eyes closed, hands acting

out each syllable. "We belong to the sound
of the words we've both fallen under,"
she smiles at her prince, her husband, playing guitar.

Ask the Angels

Arms raised like a sorcerous,
hypnotic fingers conjuring the crowd, dangly
charm bracelets, Patti's voice thunders

from the gut, "She is benediction /
She is addicted to he / She is the root connection
and / She is connecting to me."

Mid-song security can't hold back
the front rows, so Patti hops off-stage: "Settle down,
man. Get cool. Settle the fuck down.

Stop acting like assholes and settle
the fuck down," Patti coos into the mic, punk
poet laureate, future wife, mother,

widow, and winner of the National Book
Award: "The writer is conductor," drawls a cowpoke,
Patti's alter ego, a theoretical,

Sam Shepard presence of thought
in *M Train*, her memoir, security guards dispersing,
and then she submits, kneels like a prayer,

one hand extended, which brings order
and melody back to 1979, dancing barefoot, the blur-
space between rock music, poetry, and time,

that crinkly inventive universe amid
waking and dreaming and singing a life written down,
Arthur Rimbaud with Marshall amps,

electric guitars as metaphors, drums
as line breaks as confessions as onomatopoeia
as aria to a black, favorite coat.

It's Not Unusual

Over a million spectators outside
Buckingham Palace and lining The Mall,
Flamenco beats overlooking

London. "I saw the light on the night
that I passed by her window," Sir Tom Jones,
72, wooly grey hair,

testifies at Diamond Jubilee
of Queen Elizabeth II, a multi-national,
four-day celebration which marks

the 60th anniversary of her accession
to the throne, the stage sprawling, extravagant.
"I saw the flickering shadow of love

on her blind." Knighted for services
to music Sir Tom Jones makes a fist, thrusts
the knife, and during his career,

not including affairs with Mary
Wilson of the Supremes and Elvira, Mistress
of the dark,

Jones had sex with over 250 groupies
a year and somehow stayed married to Linda,
his high school sweetheart.

"My, my, my, Delilah / Why, why,
why Delilah," princes Henry and William sing
along, Union Jacks waving.

Supernatural

Vic Chesnutt's busted hands strum
simple chords that buzz
like bees. "I am a man," his voice swarms

the small-town school auditorium,
"I am self-aware."
A car accident left Chesnutt paralyzed

when he was 19, a quadriplegic
from the neck down, he jokes
during a *Fresh Air* interview with Terry Gross

at NPR. "And everywhere I go / You're
always right there with
me," Chesnutt's wheelchair-Americana

honeys the sting, but not the facts
of a man disarrayed, trapped in
a prison of skin and song. "I flirted with you

all my life / Even kissed you once or
twice / Oh death, oh death, oh
death / You're cruel, and you are constant."

High Flying Bird

Sweat soaked pantaloons and body
shirt, Richie Havens dances all around the
stage after playing for nearly three

hours, tranced, strumming, driving
his acoustic guitar to the edge of brink,
Woodstock, 1969, the festival's

first performer; Ravi Shankar, Arlo
Guthrie, Joan Baez, and the other opening
acts—stuck in traffic—are waiting

to be airlifted in from Stewart Air-
force Base; the highways and roads to
Yasgur's dairy farm, a state

of emergency according to Governor
Nelson Rockefeller who wants 10,000 New
York State National Guard troops

deployed. *Buy No Milk. Stop Max's
Hippy Music Festival*, proclaim handmade
signs from Poughkeepsie to Kingston,

but nothing can stop history, three days
of peace, melody, or Richie Haven's out of
original music, channeling energy

from his Blackfoot, Siksika grandfather
and riffing on an old slave song, "Freedom
Freedom Freedom Freedom

Freedom Freedom / Sometimes I feel
like a motherless child / Sometimes I feel like
a motherless child / Sometimes I

feel like a motherless child / A long
way from my home," and 400,000 people,
sprawled over 15 acres of green

rolling hills, la conga rhythms shining,
stand united after two crushing decades of
war and butch-waxed-crewcuts.

Let it Go

There is rain there are clouds there
is delight there is wind there is fog there is
courage there is snow

there is hot there is risk there is
yearning there is thunder there is Gaelynn
Lea, weatherworn, pitch-pine

floorboards creaking, raspy,
Celtic strains on a classically trained violin
looped live, and an orange micro-

amp singing, "We pulled the weeds
out till the dawn / Nearly too tired to carry
on / Someday we'll linger in the sun."

Gaelynn Lea has Osteogenesis
Imperfecta, a unique variety of brittle bone
disease that transmutes pain

into melodies, into twisted bow string
limbs molded for playing fiddle, like a mini-
cello, from an electric wheelchair.

"And I love you," she laments, a
glassmith freeblowing sound into gorgeous
moments of light.

Fox Hunting

Polly Jean leathers
up to the microphone, sheela
na gigs live at Reading

Festival.

Ruby lipstick vines
twist and twine, grope her
Gibson guitar string

thighs.

"I've been trying
to show you over and over," she
arouses a 12th century

superstition.

"Look at these my child
bearing hips," she marshals
a throbbing mosh pit

to Kilpeck

church, a naked woman
figurine carved into the doorway,
hands on plump legs

splayed.

The vulva is primordial,
the mysterious divide between
nonlife

and life.

"Gonna take my hips
to a man who cares," Polly Jean's
beats titillate, hunter,

hunted, goddess.

Water's Edge

"I love you
so much. I will
never forget

you," a note
wilts with a pile
of flowers

at Ovingdean
Gap where his
twin brother

fell sixty feet
after tripping on
LSD.

A woman
driving-by and
a software

designer biking
home from work
watched

Arthur Cave
zigzagging in the
leggy grass,

looking out
to sea for answers,
provoking the

unknown parts
of the untouched
depths of the

soul as Nick
his father, black,
hotwired hair

pushed back,
plumbs the piano
singing it true,

"It's a wonderful,
wonderful life / If
you can find it."

Telling Stories

Tom Waits pedals
an upright piano, tinkers
with the keys.

"This is a song
my dad taught me as a kid,"
he says

to the audience.
After a pause he admits, solemn
as a fedora, "That's a lie."

"This is a song
I learned from the kids
in the alley

behind the theater,"
his eyes are closed, he smirks
convincingly,

con-artist-extraordinaire.
After a pause he nods, deadpan,
"That's a lie too."

"I learned this song
from Gregory Peck," and the
crowd laughs harder.

"That too is a lie;
they're all lies; the whole song's
a lie."

After a pause he pianos
a vat of smokehouse bourbon
and rails, "The bats are in

the belfry / The dew is on
the moor / Where are the arms
that held me? / And

pledged her love
before? / And pledged her love
before?"

Keep it Open

The roads in Mozambique
after 25 years are deep rutted trenches,
the legacy of war and landmines.

"It's quiet now, just crickets,
and a dog fight somewhere in the far-
away," Bruce Cockburn plays

the ruined landscape on a dobro,
scratchy, tin rain falling dark clouds rolling
rough seas.

In 1959, Bruce fell in love with sound,
a dusty guitar he found in his grandmother's
attic, where he could trek all over

the world, kicking out dull habits
of mind, playing along to hits on the radio,
mellow vibraphone jazz,

mountains rising in smoke, East
African children dancing, flickering neon
towns, and swooping crows.

"If I had wings like those," Bruce
sings for the restless and the traveled who
weary the wind, and the coming rains.

Through the Years

Country Music
Hall of Famer Kenneth
Rogers, as he was

originally billed,
announced retirement
plans on *Today*.

"I've done this long
enough," says the 78 year
old icon getting ready

for his final world
tour after five marriages
and six children.

"You've got to know
when to hold 'em / Know
when to fold 'em

Know when to walk
away / And know when
to run," he smiles

warm as a straight
flush daydreaming about
spending more time

with his twin boys
and wife. "Sometimes there
is a fine line between

being driven and
being selfish," he pokers
a Texas smile.

Single Women

Tale of insecurity, red-
headed bank clerk flirts on
your husband at his

local branch; you confront
her, hands on hips, curves like
church; growing up dirt

poor, north of the Smoky
Mountains, you fingerpicked
switchbacks, rapid as

vibrato, on a homemade
guitar. "He talks about you in
his sleep / There's nothing

I can do to keep / From crying
when he calls your name, Jolene,"
your soprano is big-country

music holding the light
of day, fourth child of seven
brothers and four sisters.

Almost Real

Reading Festival on Little John's Farm
is packed, over 50,000 onlookers grooving, grinding,
Henry Rollins unleashed, "No time for drug

addiction / No time for smoke and booze / Too
strong for a shortened life span / I've got no time to lose."
Growing up a divorced kid you learn

to survive by howling back at the doomed faces
of depression; by lifting weights heavier than Ritalin
you defeat the crippling stigma of sexual

assault; by miracle the stage is home—black shorts,
bare chest, bare feet, post-punk, jazz-funk, you lunge, you
lurch, you growl, "No

such thing as spare time / No such thing as free
time / No such thing as down time / All you got is life
time . . . go!"

Silver Machine

Mutton chopped Lemmy squares off
with the mic, sited so he is looking up at the sky—
vast, familiar, total—not the audience.

"Out of the night comes a song that I know,"
his voice is Jack Daniel's, disorder, warts, honesty,
"Twisted and ruined and black."

Hell-bent Lemmy flaunted his mother's guitar
at school to impress girls even though he couldn't play;
and he wasn't shredding bass-lines yet,

or singing lead vocals when he joined
Hawkwind, but that's where he wrote, "Motorhead."
"I woke up insane today / Dreamed I was

blown away," he serenades the crowd
Live in Toronto, speed metal pioneer who loved
The Beatles and perfect ballads.

A No and a Yes

Complex, muffled cardboard box beats,
accordion bellows wheezing, falling down a
flight of stairs like a Slinky,

the music of permanent non-musical
damage of nurses at St. Ann's who delivered lumbar
punches, blunt surgical needles sucking

spinal fluid, dancing, headaches, coma,
synth loops, memory loss that deletes language,
the chaos between the unnamable

and its expression. "I like the chorus
and the postcard scenery," Johnny Lydon sings
happy-go-luckily, caned and bullied

at school because meningitis came
from the rats, warm party vibes, the sun setting over
Venice Beach.

Pale Blue Eyes

"I've come to hate
my body," Lou Reed's
weedy voice sings

on stage in Paris
dressed in funeral black,
belly swollen

from liver transplant
trauma. "If I could walk
away from me,"

his raw monotone
poetry pleads, "what do
you think I'd see?"

My Lady Story

Every note, every
spark of sound that informs
Anohni's lips,

is a miracle of daylight,
1000 suns trembling, staccato
rhythms rising

in her, making music.
"If it be your will," she opens
for the microphone,

sings a portrait, arms
breezy pine sprills, fingers mute
piano chords, recalling

when people didn't have
words. Like dream, clearcut,
forest, crisis, self.

Soul Comes Home

"I'm runnin' / I'm tryin'
to make 100 / Cause 99 & a half
it won't do," Mavis Staples

rhythms and blues for civil
rights, a bottomless spiritual voice
of faith, of harmony, of slow

motion drumbeating fists
grooving to the timbres of history,
red splashy blouse, gold

bouncy earrings, and electric
Mississippi delta bottleneck slide
guitar limning cotton rich

memories of soil and poverty:
*Brothers in jail, Uneducated children,
Broken levees, Lyin' politicians*

*running for hatred, Homeless
babies,* "Freedom now, Freedom
now, Freedom now

in a weary land," Mavis Staples
sings message songs, "Cause 99 &
a half just won't do."

Bad Reputation

"Ow," Joan Jett sandblasts
the audience, skintight black leather
jumpsuit, Barbie doll

blue eyeliner, Gibson Melody
Maker guitar slung low, hips grinding,
sweaty tattoos. "I love rock

& roll," Jett strips down words
bare as breath, bare as spit and sound,
"So come an' take your time

an' dance with me," she winks,
devoted to the ruckus pursuit of perfect,
three-chord, beer chugging truths—

after the show Jett sells Blackhearts
records out the trunk of her producer's
1980s, spoke-rimmed Cadillac.

Cherish the Day

Lusty voluptuous barefoot
night Sade medicines what hurts
deep inside. "I gave you all

the love I got / I gave you
more than I could give," she admits,
uncomplicates the stars,

tight white dress, red lacy
bustier, humid, live Brazil, 2011,
strobe-lights whirling, smooth

soul-flying, contralto jazz.
Reclusive after decades of multi-
platinum hit songs, and a

Grammy, Helen Folasade
Adu, finds success in a crumbling
English cottage at Cotswold,

a region of exceptional beauty,
because she trusts artistic integrity
above fame, because *honor*

confers a crown means
Folasade in Yoruba, the language
of her southwestern Nigeria.

Slow River

Blackstrap molasses
whole-notes and maelstrom
saxophone the stage.

"Sharks patrol these
waters," Mark Sandman low
rocks a two-string slide

bass guitar dredged
in cornmeal and deep-fried.
"Don't let your fingers

dangle in the water," his
poetry Burroughs of Kerouac
and Ginsberg.

"Don't you worry about
the day glow life preserver,"
a snare drum tick-tick-

ticks. "It won't save
you, it won't save you," Mark
reassures the crowd.

Let Me Fall in Love

NPR posters on the wall,
stray windowlit applause, floor
to ceiling shelves—curios,

cds, boxsets of sound;
Marketa sits at a Motif, Yamaha
synthesizer; she pianos

a traditional Iranian song,
Tiny Desk Concert, squared earrings,
gold necklace, red sweater;

a daf player keeps time,
goatskin stretched over a hardwood
frame, metal jingly ringlets;

"Ajab giso besane barge boo
dokhar ghoochani," Marketa sings
in Farsi, fragrant sweetbay

magnolias. "Mishkofe gol
an misashe gol dokhar ghoochani,"
familiar, new love.

Only Love

Raw emotion
Andra Day inspires
the soft-lit stage

at Austin City
Limits, prays for the
grieving families

of the Orlando
victims, three hours
of terror, the

deadliest mass
shooting by a single
shooter

in the United
States: Omar Mateen,
screaming bullets

and vengeance
for the airstrikes in
Iraq and Syria,

killed 49 people
and wounded 53 others
inside Pulse,

a night club. I'll
rise up / Rise like the
day / I'll rise

up / In spite of
the ache / I will rise
a thousand times

again," Andra
points the microphone.
"And we'll rise

up," the crowd
sings along. "Rise like
the waves / We'll

rise up / In spite of
the ache / And we'll do it
a thousand times

again / For you,"
Andra hits a polar note,
bright as Polaris.

God

No piano, no percussion,
no guitars, no live-backup-band,
yet a slender blade of light

cracks open, then another.
"Me and a gun / And a man / On
my back," sings Tori Amos,

a cappella, snarled lips, the
youngest student ever admitted
to the Peabody Conservatory

of Music. After performing
a short set, a man from the bar,
who asks for a ride home,

abducts and tortures her
for hours, threatens to cut and
take her biting and kicking

to his drughead friends. Since
she was three, Tori has perceived
sound as color, where the earth

is love, not hatred. "And do
you know Carolina," she pleads,
"Where the biscuits are

soft and sweet / These things
go through your head / When there's
a man on your back / And you're

pushed flat on your stomach,"
singing hymns, singing, *Holy, holy*
as he buttons down his pants.

Don't Explain

Written as a protest
poem Billie Holiday prays
with eyes closed

for the lynching to end
as piano keys remember
the impossible,

a father, who abandoned her
as an infant, and the 1930 incident
in Marion, Indiana,

a mob of white men break
into the city jail using sledge-
hammers; they beat

and hang two black
suspects from nearby poplar
trees: "Here is a fruit

for the crows to pluck / For
the rain to gather, for the wind to
suck / For the sun to rot,

for the tree to drop / Here
is a strange and bitter crop,"
young Billie Holiday's

slow, bluesy jazz crushes
the ginned, cigarette choked
room at Café Society,

Greenwich Village chic,
where waiters stop all service
for the *scent of magnolias.*

Last Goodbye

I am from nowhere, Jeff Buckley's blond Fender
Telecaster seems to say, reverbing a slow, dreamy
Monday night jam, tender as a trance;

center stage at café Sin-e is improvised, an area
where tables are cleared against the wall. "Southern
trees bear a strange fruit," Buckley's trembling

tenor voice as instrument arrives a cappella,
under the influence of sound, texture, and grace
notes. "Blood on the leaves and blood

at the root," scuffed boots sink in the slack Miss-
issippi River channel; and he paddles in over his head
singing, Led Zeppelin's, "Whole Lotta Love,"

when the wake from a passing tugboat pulls him
under, like the overdose of heroin that killed his father—
also, an avant-garde singer-songwriter.

"Pastoral scene of the gallant South / The bulgin'
eyes and the twisted mouth," Jeff's corpse is spotted
after six nights, twisted in the yellow swamp lilies.

Urge for Going

"Blue," Joni paints outside the lines,
canvas and colors and broad brushstrokes of language,
her mother tongue.

"Songs are like tattoos," Joni draws
a doghouse in second grade, draws herself above
average, forges an identity: Artist.

"Ink on a pin / Underneath the skin," Joni
sketches a wren of self-worth, as good as the bluebirds,
kids in row A, long flowing blond hair,

white gown, pitch black polio
scarred stage, moody, open-tuned piano—in 1965,
fragmented and penniless,

Joni surrenders her daughter for adoption,
quits art school, and sings, "An empty space to fill in,"
as if to bludgeon the yearning.

"When you see yourself in the music," Joni explains
during an interview, her honeyed voice willow charcoal,
now, "the communication is complete."

Sh-Boogie Bop

Prince grooves
on a purple guitar, live, MTV's classic
acoustic set.

Flared lapels he sings,
"This is it / It's time for you to go
to the wire."

Prince Rogers, a pianist
for the jazz group, Prince Rogers Trio,
named his son Prince

because he wanted
him to achieve mega-music-stardom;
"I wrote this song standing

in front of the mirror,"
Prince flicks a souvenir guitar pick.
"I'm serious,"

he flirts mid-solo,
and his fans erupt in funk machine unison,
"Ain't nobody better."

Blood

"Peace, peace / When
there's no peace," Sinead sings
from an artesian well

of ten thousand splendors
and ten thousand sighs. "I have
taken an overdose,"

she Facebooks
a desperate suicide-note in a
hotel room in Ireland,

guitar strings, chords,
controversy, live at Vicar Street:
"I wanna make / Something

beautiful," Sinead sings
alone on stage, wailing religiosity,
blending texture

and tension into three-part
harmonies, the only medicine
that helps. And God.

Closing Time

Mandolin, violin, fedora, tailored-
black-suit-Renaissance-Man, and three
red robins singing into one mic

Leonard Cohan is on his knees
at Mt. Baldy Zen Center after five years
in seclusion; Jikan, which means

silence, is his Dharma name. "Love
is to overlook and forgive," Cohen's voice
relaxes, finds an easy way to discuss

self-reform. "It's not a cry
that you hear at night / It's not somebody
who's seen the light / It's a cold

and it's a broken Hallelujah," he sings
in Halifax, all his money gone, retirement
accounts and charitable trust funds

embezzled by a close friend. Getting
older, he says, in defiance of body decay,
a life-long depression has lifted.

32 Flavors

"I stand here as a testament to antibiotics
and steroids too," Ani banters with the audience,
Santa Cruz.

The stage is backdrop, tinted blue
silk curtains, and aerosol-sprayed spotlights frame
the microphone.

"We're going back to the bad old days,"
Ani laughs, now, cracks open fists of geodes
on the acoustic guitar, drumming

geological notes, staccato picking fingers
prizing out the crystals, chords like sculptures,
Venus de Milo's first words.

"life use to be lifelike / now it's more like
showbiz / I wake up in the night / and I don't know
where the bathroom is," Ani eases

into the microphone as if easing into a
microphone is the most natural thing in the world
to ease into, like busking in Buffalo

with her guitar teacher when she was nine,
or playing Beatles covers at local bars and coffee
houses during her teens, already living alone,

emancipated from her parents,
and planning a self-titled debut with Righteous Babe
Records, a company she will found.

"every song has a you / a you that the singer
sings to / and you're it this time / baby, you're it
this time,"

and the crowd cheers a catharsis of
goddess energy, Ani as deity, Brooklyn as refuge,
silkscreened red on a gray sleeveless t-shirt.

Talking with the Wolves

Still-life mandolin on the table, Sennheiser
headphones, cans of Schweppes seltzer, a foghorn
whistle, gnarled warbler nest of wires

plugged into studio-microphones, Google
Chrome gawking computer screens, and the Opie
Radio crew at SiriusXM mesmerized

by the light, nimbus guitar and Glen Hansard
sailing into the majestic, soul and spirit flying, singing,
"We were born before the wind / Also younger

than the sun," and when there's nothing
but music in your head, and you *hear the sailors
cry*, and *smell the sea and feel the sky*,

nothing makes more sense than quitting school
at 13 to busk on the streets of Dublin, covering songs
by the holy trinity: Cohen, Dylan, Morrison.

No Guru, No Method, No Teacher

A slow sailing saxophone, moody-blue lights,
fedora, pinstripes, sunglasses, guitar strings fading
into aquatic sounds on piano,

electric bass thrumming like a boat in motion,
water as a means of transformation, and you feel
every grace note, every influence

his father's record collection inspired: Jelly
Roll Morton, Ray Charles, Lead Belly, Muddy Waters,
Mahalia Jackson, Charlie Parker, Woody Guthrie,

Hank Williams. "And when that foghorn blows
I will be coming home / And when that foghorn blows
I want to hear it / I don't want to fear it," Van

Morrison sails around Lyric Theatre, his mother,
Violet, singing and tap dancing around the record player
console when she was young.

Sentimental Hygiene

"Shadows are falling, and
I'm running out of breath / Keep me
in your heart for a while,"

Warren Zevon, son of a Russian
gangster, sings farewell, diagnosed
with inoperable peritoneal

mesothelioma from asbestos from
the attic at his father's carpet store,
where he daydreamed Brahms,

Stravinsky, and Mozart concertos
before quitting high school for the New
York City, folk revival scene.

"When you get up in the morning
and you see that crazy sun / Keep me
in your heart for a while," sings

death and dying in the key of G,
in the key of Warren Zevon strumming
along with his guitar of drugs and

alcohol, of rehab and relapse, of
libretto, recovery, and cremation, Zevon's
ashes mixed with the ocean near his

home in Los Angeles, where he
refused cancer treatment for the love
of ham and cheese sandwiches

and to write, "There's a train leaving
nightly called, 'When all is said and done'
keep me in your heart for a while."

Hero in Me

Tin walls painted red
halfway up the squat ceiling;
polished oak panels

soaked in local beer;
smoky limelight; scratchy
metamorphosis voice;

and drinkers at the bar
and sitting at tables talking
over an acoustic set,

live at Gullifty's as Jeffrey
Gaines rocks Aretha Franklin,
Gladys Knight & the Pips,

and Maya Angelou,
"I was gathering all the things
I had to tell you / And

found that there were more
things I had to hide / Like lovers
and tears, doubts and fears

inside me / Cause when
you're away," the drunk, 12 a.m.
crowd finally sings along,

"There's nothing to say
at all / Cause when you're not
here / Love disappears."

Beeswing

Symphony in six strings
Richard Thompson troubadours
Texas, living the landscape

of Django Reinhardt jazz, of
the Great Highland pipers plotting
war, of Jerry Lee's great balls

of fire, of Shetland fiddles, tin
whistles, country-dance accordions,
of Gaelic house harps, of boggy

woodwose rhythms, and black
magical chords chanting as he sings
smoky peat tones, "Said James,

'In my opinion, there's nothing
in this world / Beats a '52 Vincent
and a Redheaded girl.'"

Psycho Killer

"Un di felice,
eterea," David Bryne
Italians the mic,

a lanky pop
Pavarotti, studded
gray hair, Gibson

guitar, and ears
plugged so he can hit
perfect La Traviata

pitch; the stage
at Union Chapel is
stained glass,

lavish medieval
lines, scallops, finials,
lancet windows.

"One day, happy,
ethereal," violins and
cello coax a

poignant tenor
from Byrne's airy
falsetto, and the

crowd, rapt, gets
the story: Violetta tells
Alfredo to find

somebody else,
and Byrne responds
as Alfredo as a

man devoured as
Talking Heads at their
Rock & Roll Hall

of Fame induction,
burning down the house,
gut strings, arpeggio,

and Asperger's,
fingers saying what
the voice cannot.

Metamorphosis

Head bowed, hands praying,
piano is cathedral at the Garrison
Institute, where wizards and

leaders contemplate the sunset
in three acts: I. massive, hazy fireball
disappears below the horizon;

II. illuminated wind-shear clouds
separate orange from blue, separate
self from body from ideology,

crickets singing a distant calling
song; III. classicist Philip Glass studies
flute as a boy and attends

Julliard to embody sound, tones
without reason, mad rush of harmony,
refuge, counter / point, Bach

Mozart, dusk. Is the very end
of twilight, the darkest, peaceable
moment, then night.

∞

CODA

∞

The Music Never Ends

London Palladium is packed,
over 2000 seats, Tony Bennett's favorite
theater, and as proof

he tells the sound man to switch
off all the mics, and then he launches
into outer space, a cappella.

"Poets often say simple things / To
make a feeling," Tony Bennett is Joe Bari,
his stage name before WWII,

or he's 13 again, performing
as a singing waiter at Italian restaurants
around his native Queens, NY.

"With music and words / I've been
playing / For you," he claps and pure joy
lights his face, brown eyes smiling

over the audience. "Fly me
to the moon," Bennett's arm is a rocket
ship, and contrails of cheers erupt

from his fingers, 85 years old, top
40 hits, marriages, grandkids, drug abuse,
gold and platinum records.

"Fill my heart with song / And let
me sing forevermore," he belts it out across
the universe as easily as breathing,

textures of sound, layers of pure
emotions, mixed media on canvas: ribbon,
metal, wood, lace, leather, sand.

About the Author

Gary Rainford, author of the poetry collection, *Salty Liquor*, lives on Swan's Island year-round with his wife and daughter. Gary's suite of poems, *We Are Here*, was an honorable mention selected by Betsy Sholl for The Gabriel Zimpritch Memorial Poetry Prize. His poems, shaped by tides, saltwater, and music, are published in a wide range of literary magazines, university journals, and newspapers. *Liner Notes*, says Gary, is a tribute to great songs, inspired musicians, poetic form, his love of singing in the shower, and playing acoustic, air-guitar. Connect with Gary at www.garyrainford.com.

www.ingramcontent.com/pod-product-compliance
Lightning Source LLC
Chambersburg PA
CBHW030003050426
42451CB00006B/101